Science and Technology
Medical Technology

Ann Fullick

Chicago, Illinois

www.heinemannraintree.com
Visit our website to find out
more information about
Heinemann-Raintree books.

To order:
☎ Phone 888-454-2279
💻 Visit www.heinemannraintree.com
to browse our catalog and order online.

Edited by Andrew Farrow, Adam Miller, and Diyan Leake
Designed by Victoria Allen
Original illustrations © Capstone Global Library Ltd 2012
Illustrated by Oxford Designers and Illustrators
Picture research by Elizabeth Alexander
Originated by Capstone Global Library Ltd
Printed and bound in China by CTPS

15 14 13 12 11
10 9 8 7 6 5 4 3 2 1

Library of Congress Cataloging-in-Publication Data
Fullick, Ann, 1956-
  Medical technology / Ann Fullick.
    p. cm.—(Sci-Hi: science and technology)
  Includes bibliographical references and index.
  ISBN 978-1-4109-4273-9 (hc)—ISBN 978-1-4109-4282-1
(pb) 1. Medical technology. 2. Medical innovations. I.
Title.
  R855.3.F85 2012
  610.28—dc22   2010054325

Acknowledgments
The author and publishers are grateful to the following
for permission to reproduce copyright material:
Alamy pp. **4** (© Mike Hill), 5 (© Medical-on-Line), **8**
(© wonderlandstock), **11** (© Spencer Grant), **13** (© Ace
Stock Limited), **25** (© doc-stock), **34** (© Melba Photo
Agency; Corbis pp. **19** (© Howard Sochurek), **21** (© Ian
Hooton/Science Photo Library), **22** (© Andrew Winning/
Reuters), **28** (© Dung Vo Trung), **31** (© Alexandra Beier/
Reuters), **32** (© Li Ga/Xinhua Press; Getty Images pp. **6**
(SSPL), **7** (Hulton Archive), **15** (Gallo Images—Media24),
23, **33** (Brandi Simons), **36** (Tim Hale/Workbook Stock),
37 (Alvis Upitis/Brand X Pictures); Science Photo
Library pp. **9** (Moredun Animal Health Ltd), **26** (Pascal
Goetgheluck), **29** (AJ Photo/HOP American), **30** (BSIP
LECA), **35** (John McLean), **40** (Geoff Tompkinson);
Shutterstock **contents page** top (© R. Perreault),
contents page bottom (© Andrea Danti), pp. **10**
(© Skyhawk), **12** (© jason Stitt), **14** (© Condor 36), **20**
(© Alexonline), **27** (© R. Perreault), **39** (© Andrea Danti),
all background and design features.

Main cover photograph of a bionic hand reproduced
with permission of Alamy (© Steve Lindridge); inset cover
photograph reproduced with permission of shutterstock
(© Matt Ragen).

The publisher would like to thank literary consultant
Nancy Harris and content consultant Suzy Gazlay for
their assistance in the preparation of this book.

Every effort has been made to contact copyright holders
of material reproduced in this book. Any omissions will
be rectified in subsequent printings if notice is given to
the publisher.

Disclaimer
All the Internet addresses (URLs) given in this book were
valid at the time of going to press. However, due to the
dynamic nature of the Internet, some addresses may
have changed, or sites may have changed or ceased to
exist since publication. While the author and publisher
regret any inconvenience this may cause readers, no
responsibility for any such changes can be accepted by
either the author or the publisher.

Contents

How can tattoos be removed? Turn to page 27 to find out!

What is a nanobot? Read page 39 to find out!

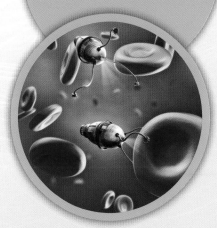

Some words are shown in bold, **like this**. These words are explained in the glossary. You will find important information and definitions underlined, <u>like this</u>.

WHAT IS MEDICAL TECHNOLOGY?

Doctors use all kinds of things to help make people better. A simple bandage can cover a small cut. A beam of light called a **laser** can improve sight. A **life-support machine** can keep a body going for a few days while someone recovers from serious illness or **surgery**. All of these are examples of medical technology.

Looking inside the body

Doctors often need to be able to see inside patients' bodies to find out what is wrong with them. Lots of medical technology is used to help. X-rays are good at showing up broken bones. **MRI scans** and **CAT (CT) scans** can show doctors any problems with the softer organs of the body, such as the liver or lungs.

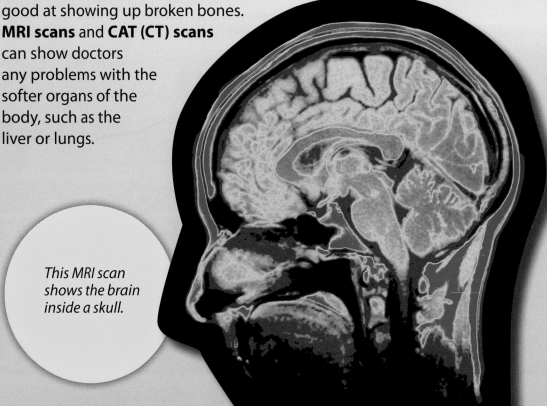

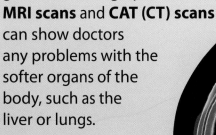

This MRI scan shows the brain inside a skull.

Keeping people alive

If people are very sick, doctors use all sorts of medical technology to keep them alive. There are machines that can breathe for people and pump the blood around the body. There are ways of giving people food when they cannot eat. Another machine can take waste materials out of the blood, so they don't poison patients. The machines that take over everything are called life-support machines.

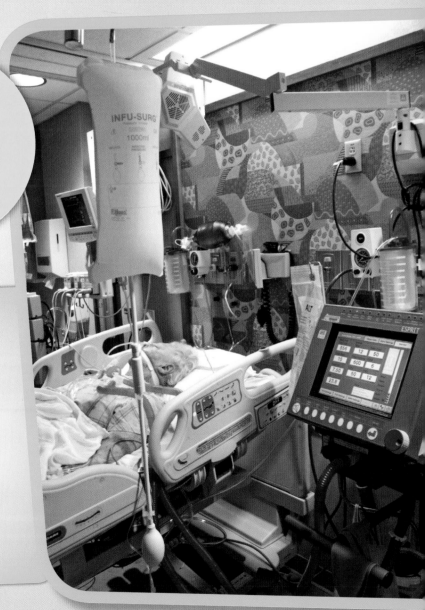

It takes a lot of technology to keep a seriously ill person alive.

In 2008 almost 38 million people in the United States went to a hospital. Most patients probably needed something to help them get better. This could range from a bandage to a life-support machine. That is a lot of medical technology.

SOME EARLY MEDICAL TECHNOLOGY

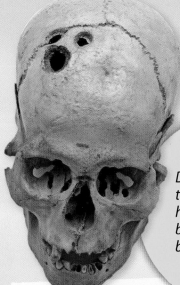

People have been using technology to try to cure diseases for thousands of years. Some early medical technology was quite frightening—and it often did not work very well.

During prehistoric times, people didn't have hospitals— but they did try brain surgery.

THE 1600s: EARLY SURGERY

For hundreds of years, surgery was only done when it was the last chance to save a life. There was no way to prevent patients from feeling pain other than giving them an alcoholic drink. Most people who lived through the pain of surgery died of **infection** (germs entering the wound) later. The best **surgeons** could take off a leg in a few minutes.

PREHISTORIC TIMES: BRAIN SURGERY

Scientists have found some prehistoric skulls with holes cut in them, a process known as **trepanning**. We know the patients survived, because bone had started to grow back over the holes. Scientists think prehistoric people were trying to cure seizures (fits of violent shaking) and headaches. They may have thought it would let evil spirits out of the skull.

PREHISTORIC

1600s

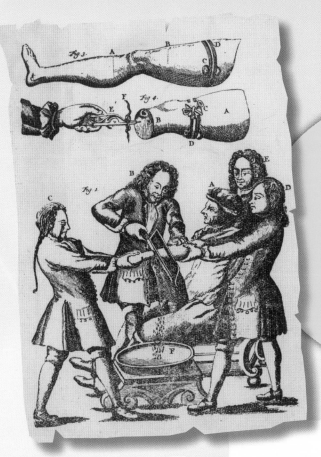

Early surgeons had to work quickly while the patient was held down. There were no painkillers in the 1750s, when this diagram was drawn.

THE 1800s: MAKING CHILDBIRTH SAFER

In the past, many women died from problems giving birth. Forceps had been invented in the 1600s, but they were not in wide use until the 1800s. Forceps are tools that can help deliver a baby safely if it gets stuck during birth. They have saved the lives of thousands of mothers and babies.

THE 1900s: THE STETHOSCOPE

The stethoscope was invented in 1816. The tubes on a stethoscope allow doctors to listen to the sound of a heart beating. Doctors can hear air moving in and out of patients' lungs when they breathe, and it helps them to detect many different diseases. A stethoscope is a simple piece of medical technology that has saved many lives.

1800s

1900s

DIAGNOSING DISEASE

If a patient is sick, a doctor needs to find out what is wrong to decide upon the best treatment. A good doctor will listen to a patient to find out what is wrong. Doctors will also use different types of medical technology to help them make a **diagnosis** (identify what exactly is wrong).

Testing the blood

Blood tests have been an important method of detecting disease for many years. Scientists create special **cells**. Cells are the very small parts that form all living things. These cells make **monoclonal antibodies**. Monoclonal antibodies are special substances that target cells in the body. They let doctors detect problems before they make someone really sick.

Pregnancy tests use monoclonal antibodies to find out if a woman is pregnant as soon as possible. Then she can get good medical care. The bars in this test shows that the woman is pregnant.

Pregnant

Not Pregnant

Using monoclonal antibodies

Monoclonal antibodies are used in many tests for the disease cancer. They can be used to screen people who show no signs of disease. Monoclonal antibodies can be used to find out which **microorganism** (tiny living thing) is causing illness. This is important, because treating cancer early gives people the best chance of getting better. This means doctors can use the right medicine to make people better.

Looking at cells

Microscopes are another important piece of medical technology. They can magnify (enlarge) very small objects hundreds of times. Using microscopes, doctors can see the changes in cells when cancers grow. They can also identify the different **bacteria** that cause infections, so that they use the right medicine. Bacteria are very tiny living things that can cause disease.

*Microscopes show doctors when cancer cells (shown here) are growing. Often a tiny sample of body tissue is taken to be checked for cancer cells under a microscope. **Electron microscopes** can magnify cells many thousands of times. They can be used to identify what is causing an infectious disease.*

Looking inside the body

To **diagnose** what is wrong with someone, doctors often need to be able to see inside the body without cutting a person open. Medical technology makes this possible.

X-rays and CAT scanners

Doctors have used X-rays for over 100 years, but they are still the quickest way to see a broken bone. X-rays are created by using a special type of light. The light passes through the soft parts of the body, but it is stopped by hard tissue like bones and teeth. So, it is just hard tissue that shows up in a photograph. We call the special photograph that shows these bones an X-ray.

CAT, or CT, scanners use X-rays and computers to make lots of images of slices through the body. These pictures are very clear. Computers put all the information together to make a complete 3-D image of a person's insides. Doctors can use these images to diagnose many problems, from brain **tumors** (cancer lumps) to heart disease.

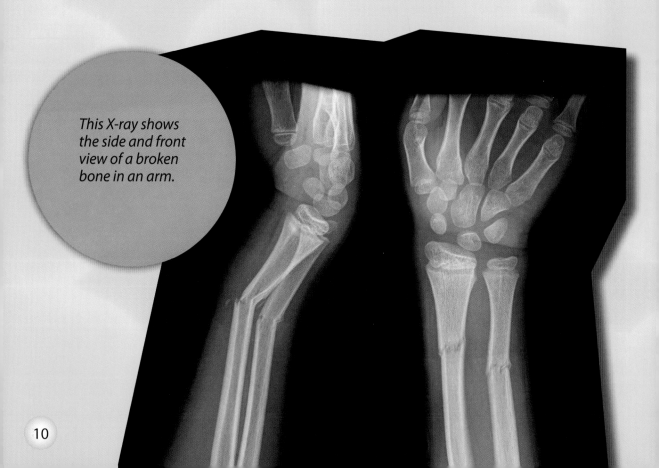

This X-ray shows the side and front view of a broken bone in an arm.

WHO DID THAT?
X-RAYS

X-rays were first discovered in 1895 by Wilhelm Röntgen, when he was investigating vacuum tubes. He called them X-rays because he didn't know what they were.

MORE WAYS OF SEEING INSIDE PEOPLE

- Doctors also use ultrasound. This is sound that is too high for humans to hear. Ultrasound can go through the body.

- MRI scans give a detailed picture of the inside of the body. They are very safe to use. MRI scans are used to help doctors diagnose many different diseases.

- Endoscopes are tiny cameras that can be put inside the body. They can be used to help identify problems within the body. They can even be used to perform surgery.

- PET imaging lets doctors find very small areas of cancer. It is also good for seeing inside the brain.

A CAT scanner is a big machine with a tunnel in the middle. The patient lies on a table that slides in and out of this tunnel. It doesn't take many minutes to get images of the whole body.

MEDICINES

Medicines can make people better, or at least more comfortable. They can also protect people from disease. Doctors use **vaccines** (often through shots) to "teach" the body how to attack bacteria and **viruses** (microorganisms that cause disease). People can swallow a medicine in pill form. Some medicines need special technology to get inside the body.

Asthma attack

Asthma is a common problem in children and adults. In an asthma attack, the lining of the tubes that carry air down into the lungs swells up. The muscles around the tubes tighten, and the airways become smaller. This makes it difficult to get air in and out of the lungs. It is important to get medicine into the lungs fast to relax the muscles and reduce the swelling—and to help the person breathe.

Medicine for the lungs

Asthma medicine is delivered using an inhaler, which goes in the mouth. It gives a spray of medicine that is breathed down into the lungs. Nebulizers make a medicine mist that is then breathed in through a mask.

Inhalers are used to give medicines to relieve asthma symptoms. They can also be used daily to give medicine that makes asthma attacks less likely.

Injecting medicine

Some medicines need to be given straight into the blood or the muscles. This is often done by injections, pumps, or drips. Some people have an illness called diabetes. Their bodies are unable to make the chemical insulin. Insulin is needed to help the cells get the sugar from the blood.

Some people with diabetes (called diabetics) need to inject themselves with insulin several times a day. A new way of treating diabetes is with an insulin pump. This pump puts insulin under the skin all the time. More and more people are using these pumps.

BRIGHT IDEA

Some people are allergic to a particular food or medicine. They react so strongly that their breathing and heart may stop. They carry an EpiPen all the time. EpiPens contain a chemical called adrenalin, which can be injected easily into the muscle. Adrenalin stops the allergic reaction. So, EpiPens can save lives.

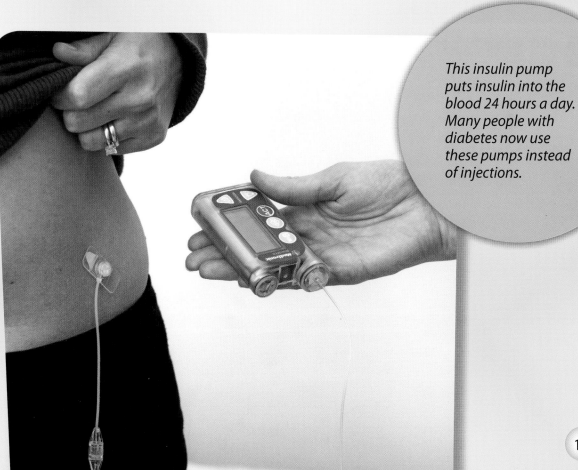

This insulin pump puts insulin into the blood 24 hours a day. Many people with diabetes now use these pumps instead of injections.

SURGERY

During surgery, doctors go inside the human body to cure diseases or mend things that are not working well. As medical technology gets better, surgeons can carry out more and more amazing operations.

A chemical sleep

Modern surgery relies on **anesthesia** (the loss of the sensation of touch through drugs). **Anesthetics** make sure patients can feel no pain during surgery. **General anesthetics** put patients into a deep sleep. Modern anesthetics are very safe. They can be injected into the blood or breathed in. Machines check for heart beat, blood pressure, and breathing while patients are in this deep chemical sleep.

Open surgery

A surgeon has to cut through the body wall to get to the organs inside. Much of the technology in the operating room is there to make the operation as safe as possible. There are special lights so the surgeon can see well. There are many different instruments to make it as easy as possible for the surgeon to work. They stop the bleeding and reduce the shock to the patient's body.

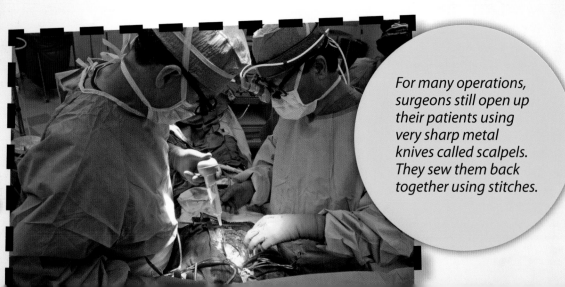

For many operations, surgeons still open up their patients using very sharp metal knives called scalpels. They sew them back together using stitches.

Cutting and sticking

Surgeons don't just use scalpels (sharp knives) anymore. Lasers and even tiny, high-pressure jets of water can be used to cut parts of the body. Stitches are still often used in surgery. But more and more surgeons use special glues to bind tissue together, since there is less bleeding. People also heal faster this way.

In laparoscopic surgery, surgeons watch what they are doing on a screen. They control the instruments from outside the body.

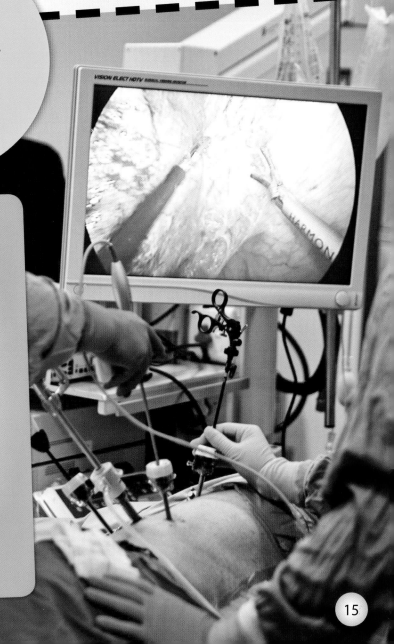

LAPAROSCOPIC SURGERY

More and more operations are done using laparoscopic surgery. The surgeon puts a tube containing a tiny camera in through the patient's belly button. The instruments needed go in through one or two more tiny holes that are made. There is no big scar to heal. Most patients recover very quickly from laparoscopic surgery.

Robotic surgery

In some hospitals, robots carry out surgery under the control of a surgeon. This robotic surgery is becoming more common. Robots can make very tiny stitches—and they never have shaky hands!

Detailed surgery

The robots used can carry out difficult and complicated surgery. The movements of a robot surgeon can be very carefully controlled. Doctors hope they will make surgery on areas like the eye, the ear, and the brain much easier and safer in the future.

Surgery at a distance

Robotic surgery has made other things possible. In 2001 a woman in Strasbourg, France, had an operation by laparoscopic surgery. The surgeons who did the operation were in the United States. This was almost 6,500 kilometers (4,000 miles) away. The robot surgeon that carried out the operation in France was controlled by an American surgeon and a French surgeon through computer links to the operating room. Many more distant operations have been done since. It means surgeons with special skills can help patients all over the world.

WHO DID THAT?
ROBOTIC SURGERY

One of the main scientists behind robotic surgery is Professor Brian Davies from the United Kingdom. In 1988 he developed the first robot ever to take tissue from a human patient. His best-known robot is used in knee surgery.

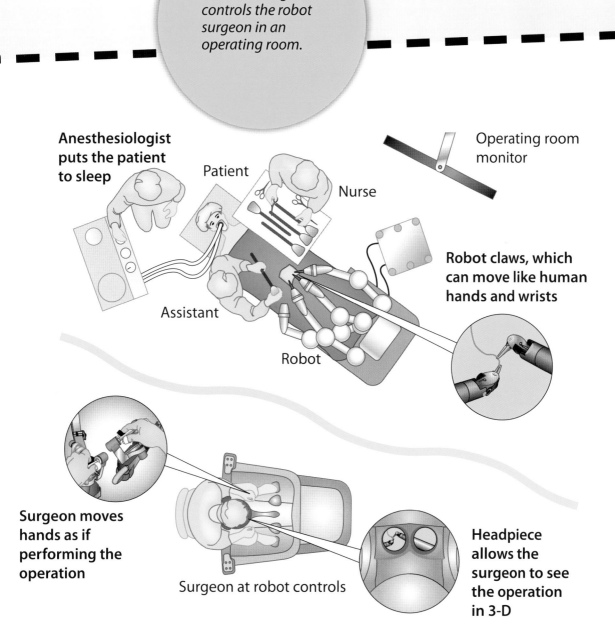

A human surgeon controls the robot surgeon in an operating room.

Anesthesiologist puts the patient to sleep

Patient

Nurse

Operating room monitor

Robot claws, which can move like human hands and wrists

Assistant

Robot

Surgeon moves hands as if performing the operation

Surgeon at robot controls

Headpiece allows the surgeon to see the operation in 3-D

Hearts, Surgery, and Technology

Heart disease causes more deaths than any other disease in countries like the United States. But some amazing technology means that doctors now have more ways to help patients with heart disease than ever before.

The human heart

The human heart is a bag of muscle. It pumps the blood to the lungs to pick up oxygen, and then it pumps it around the body. The heart beats around 60 to 70 a minute all through a person's life. It has parts cal **valves**. Valves are like doors that stop the blood from flowing in the wrong direction. The heart muscle gets a good supply of food and oxygen from the coronary **arteries** (tubes or vessels).

These common problems can all stop the heart from working properly.

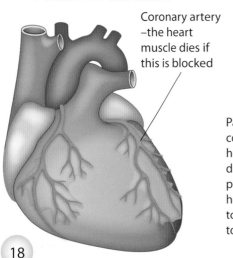

Outside of the heart

Coronary artery –the heart muscle dies if this is blocked

Inside the heart

Blood goes out to the body

Blood goes to the lungs

Valve

Pacemaker region controls the basic heartbeat–if this doesn't work properly, the heart beats too fast or too slow

Blood comes in from the body

Blood comes back from the lungs

Valve

Valve–if one of the valves stops working, blood does not flow properly through the heart

Valve

Heart problems

Lots of things can go wrong with the heart. If the coronary arteries get narrow or blocked, the heart muscle does not get the food and oxygen it needs. That can cause a heart attack. If the valves don't work properly, or the rhythm of the heart is affected, blood isn't pumped around the body properly.

Looking into the heart

If someone starts to get breathless when climbing the stairs, or gets chest pains when exercising, a doctor will want to check the person's heart. There is more than one way to look at the heart.

- An **ultrasound scan** (see page 28) can show doctors if the valves of the heart are working properly.

- A CAT (or CT) scan can show more detail of the size of the parts of the heart, and if the blood vessels are fine.

- In an **angiogram**, a special liquid that shows up on X-rays is injected into the blood. Then the heart is X-rayed, and the coronary arteries can be seen.

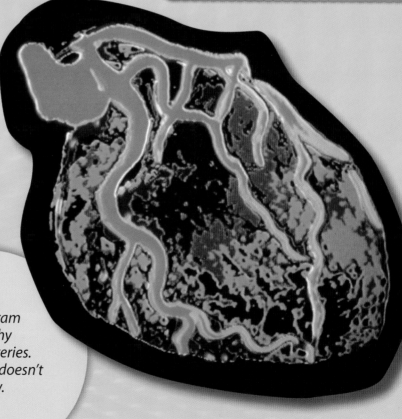

This angiogram shows healthy coronary arteries. This patient doesn't need surgery.

Bypass surgery and stents

For years doctors replaced narrow or blocked coronary arteries with pieces of veins from other parts of the body. This is called bypass surgery. It is still used, but it is expensive and needs a general anesthetic.

Today, doctors often use **stents** to open up the blood vessels, so that the blood can flow again. A stent is a metal mesh that is placed in the artery. The artery takes blood-carrying food and oxygen to different parts of the body. A tiny balloon is inflated to open up the blood vessel and the stent at the same time. Doctors can put a stent in place without a general anesthetic. Many stents also release drugs. The drugs stop the blood from clotting (thickening) and blocking up the artery.

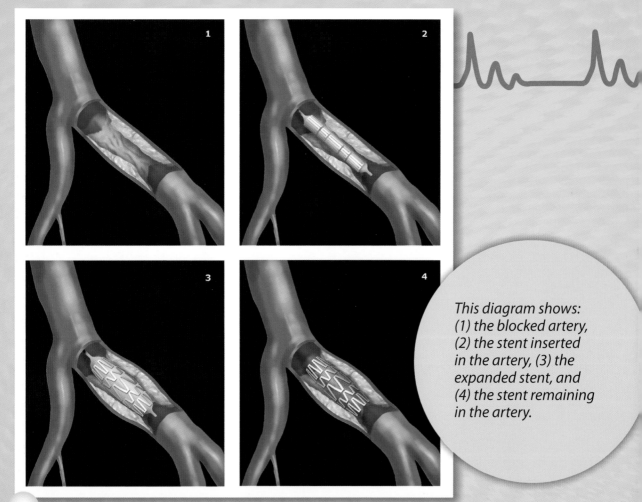

This diagram shows: (1) the blocked artery, (2) the stent inserted in the artery, (3) the expanded stent, and (4) the stent remaining in the artery.

Controlling the heart rate

If a person's heart beats much too slowly or very fast all the time, the person can feel sick. A pacemaker can be implanted under the skin, with wires going into the heart. The pacemaker gives the heart a regular, tiny electric shock so that it beats at the correct rate.

Replacing heart valves

Valves are the parts of the heart that control the flow of the blood. If they start leaking, they need to be replaced through open-heart surgery. Doctors cut through the breast bone and pull the ribs apart, to insert a new valve into the heart. The valve may be an artificial one made from plastic and metal. Or it may be a valve from an animal such as a pig or cow.

BRIGHT IDEA

If someone has a heart attack, the heart stops beating. A controlled electric shock can start the heart beating again. Defibrillators are machines that do this. They are used in hospitals, but they are also found in shopping centers, restaurants, and sports stadiums. This has helped save many lives.

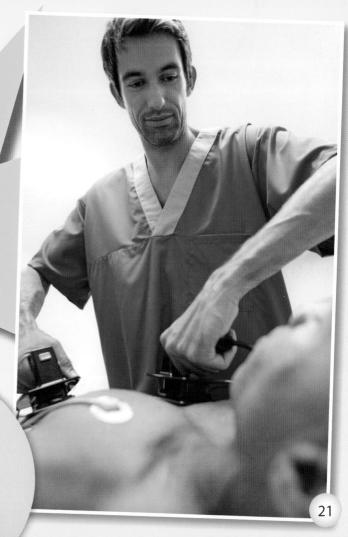

Defibrillators use an electric shock to restart a heart that has stopped.

Heart transplants

Sometimes a heart is so badly damaged or diseased that doctors cannot make it better. Then the only way to save the life of a patient is to give a heart transplant. The new heart comes from a person who has died and wished to give his or her organs to help someone else (an organ donor). The heart needs to be inserted into the new patient as quickly as possible.

Connecting the heart

The new heart needs to be kept cool in special chemicals so it is healthy and undamaged. It may travel hundreds or thousands of miles in a box from one hospital to another. The damaged heart of the patient is stopped and removed. Then the new heart is put in its place.

Hannah Clark is a girl who was given a heart transplant when she was a toddler. Her own heart was also left in place. Ten years later, the transplant was removed when Hannah's heart recovered!

Helping hearts

There are never enough donor hearts to go around. Scientists and doctors are trying to develop artificial hearts instead. LVADs (Left Ventricular Assist Devices) can help the heart to beat until it recovers and can work on its own. LVADs can also keep a diseased heart working for long enough for a donor organ to be found.

WHO DID THAT?
HEART TRANSPLANT

The first heart transplant was carried out by Dr. Christiaan Barnard in South Africa in 1967. The patient was Louis Washkansky, and the donor was 23-year-old Denise Darvall, who had died in a car accident. Louis lived for only 18 days with his new heart, but this was a medical breakthrough.

Artificial hearts

Some complete artificial hearts have been used to try to keep patients alive long enough to find an organ to transplant. There have been some successes, but also many problems with these hearts. In 2011 a team of French scientists will begin trials of a true artificial heart. They hope it will replace a diseased heart without the need for a transplant. A U.S. team is also close to developing a permanent artificial heart to try out on patients.

This was the first artificial heart designed to completely replace a human heart. The patient lived for 151 days after he received it.

LIFE SUPPORT

The cells of the body need a supply of food and oxygen all the time. The waste made by the cells is poisonous, so people need to get it out of their bodies. But during major surgery on the heart, or if someone is seriously ill, the body can't keep going. This is when medical technology takes over. A life-support machine can keep people alive.

This diagram shows the processes involved when a person is on a life-support machine.

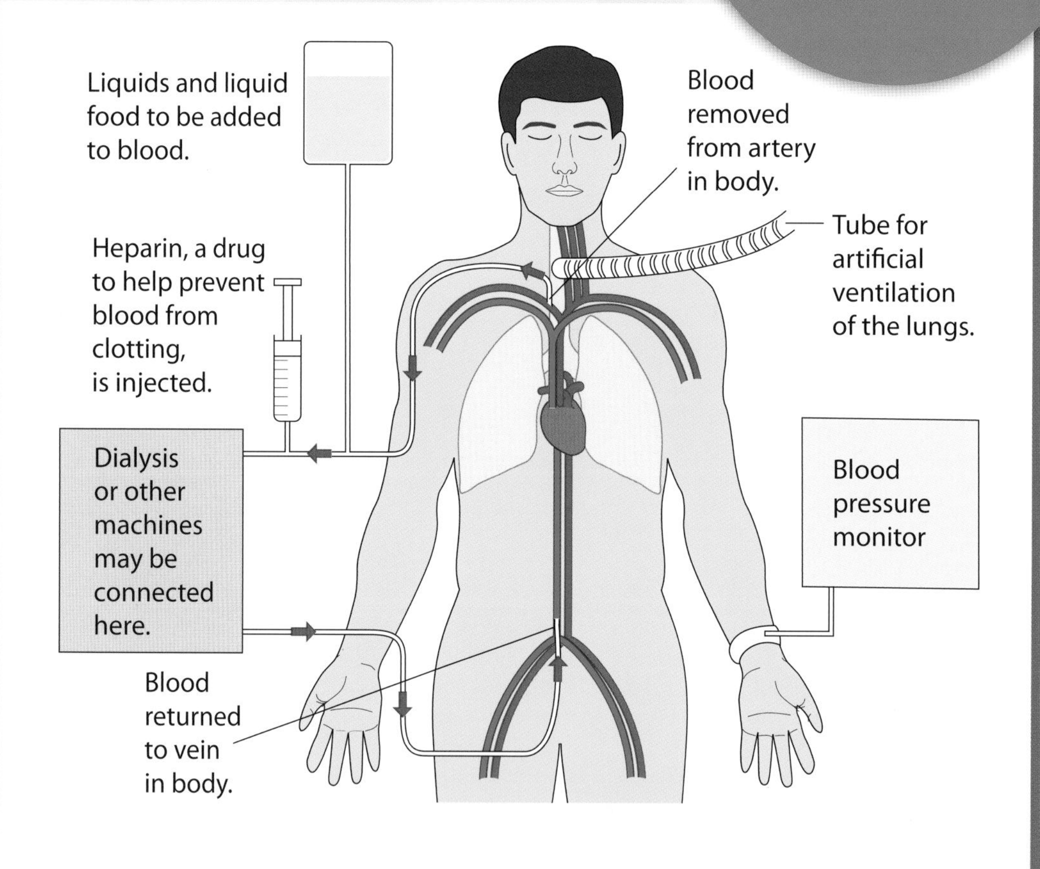

Liquids and liquid food to be added to blood.

Heparin, a drug to help prevent blood from clotting, is injected.

Dialysis or other machines may be connected here.

Blood returned to vein in body.

Blood removed from artery in body.

Tube for artificial ventilation of the lungs.

Blood pressure monitor

Life support

Different life-support machines do different jobs, according to what the patient needs. The machines can take over the job of the heart and the lungs. They can take blood out of the body and put oxygen into the blood. They also remove the waste gas carbon dioxide. They then pump the blood back into the body. The machine checks the temperature of the patient's blood and the levels of oxygen and carbon dioxide all the time. Early life-support machines were called heart–lung machines.

Kidney machines

A full life-support machine has a kidney **dialysis** machine joined on to it. This takes over the job of the kidneys. It cleans the blood by taking out waste. It also balances the levels of salt and water in the blood.

If people's kidneys don't work, they need to use a kidney dialysis machine several times a week to keep them alive and well.

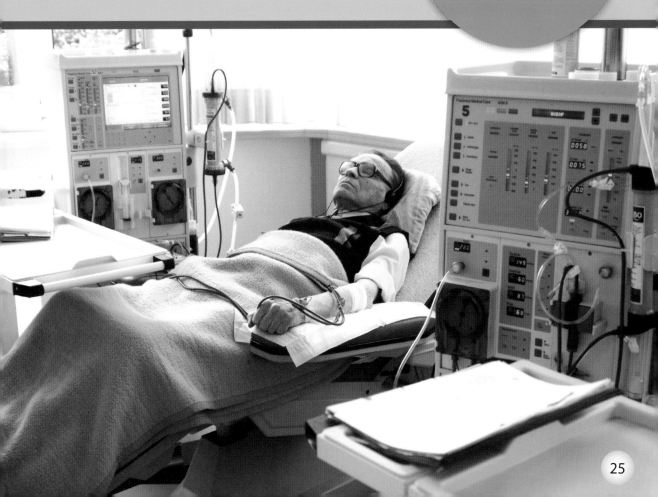

LASERS AND ULTRASOUND

Laser light is a beam of very bright light that contains lots of **energy** (power). Doctors are finding new ways to use laser technology in medicine. Ultrasound scans use sound waves to see inside the body.

Lasers and eye surgery

The light energy in a laser is all focused on a very tiny area. This makes it very hot and very accurate. Lasers are ideal for cutting and sealing wounds.

Being shortsighted means a person can see close-up but not far away, and being farsighted is the opposite. The shape of the eyeball causes these conditions. In eye surgery, doctors may use lasers to take very thin layers from the eye, to correct the shape. After laser surgery, a person would not need glasses or contact lenses anymore.

Using a laser to remove a tiny amount of tissue from the surface of the eye can give perfect vision.

Scars and tattoos

Because lasers cut away very thin layers of tissue, they can be used in plastic surgery to help remove scars and birthmarks.

Lasers and cancer

Surgeons are finding more ways to use lasers in surgery. Because lasers are so hot, they seal any blood vessels that they cut. So, laser surgery causes less bleeding. Lasers are very useful for removing cancer tumors and for destroying cancer cells. They can shrink tumors that cannot be treated in any other way, making patients more comfortable. Lasers can also be used to reach tumors deep in the brain.

FAST WORK

In laser eye surgery, each pulse of laser light removes about 0.001 millimeters (or 39 millionths of 1 inch) of the front of the eye in a few milliseconds.

Lasers are the best way to remove tattoos that people get and then regret. But even lasers leave some scarring.

Ultrasound pictures

Ultrasound scans help doctors see inside a body. Ultrasound scans also help doctors and parents watch as a baby develops. Ultrasound can show if there are one, two, or more babies. They can show if the baby's heart and the brain are growing normally. Modern ultrasound images can even be three-dimensional (3-D). The parents can see their baby's face before it is born. More importantly, doctors can see any problems as the baby develops, and so be ready to help when the baby is born.

Ultrasound and surgery

Surgeons can use ultrasound scans to build up a 3-D image of a problem before they operate. Sometimes doctors have to separate twins who are born joined together (known as conjoined twins). They need lots of 3-D ultrasound pictures to plan the surgery. **HIFU (high-intensity focused ultrasound)** can also be used in surgery. It rapidly heats and seals blood vessels to stop bleeding.

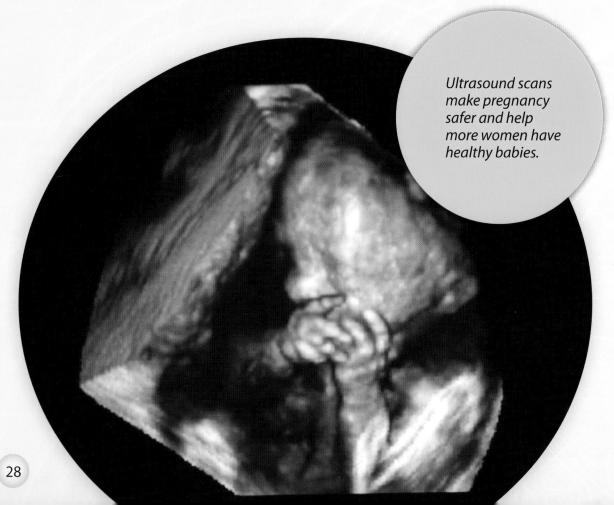

Ultrasound scans make pregnancy safer and help more women have healthy babies.

Emergency ultrasound

When soldiers are injured or there is a big disaster, people need to be treated very quickly. Doctors hope ultrasound scans and HIFU can be used in an emergency to save many lives.

Sound in action

Sometimes hard lumps can form in the kidney and bladder. These are called stones. They are very painful and must be removed. Now doctors often use sound instead of surgery. They can use ultrasound or normal sound to focus on the kidney or bladder stones. The stones shatter into tiny pieces. These then come out of the body in urine.

When sound is used to break up kidney stones, the patient stays awake the whole time.

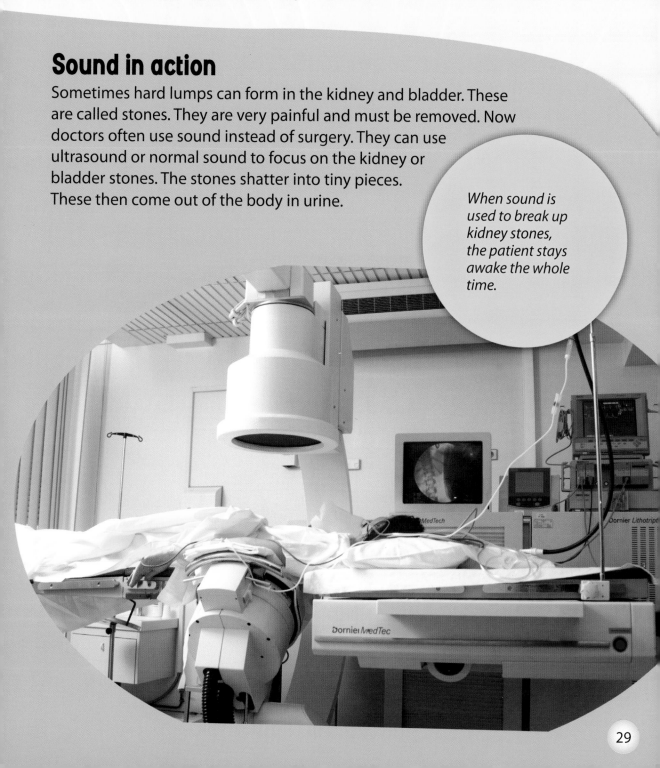

REPLACEMENT SURGERY

Sometimes people lose an organ or tissue from disease. Sometimes a limb, an organ, or the skin or blood is lost in an accident. Doctors and surgeons need to use many different types of medical technology to save these patients.

Blood donation

In any operation, patients may bleed a lot. People can lose a lot of blood in accidents, too. If people lose too much blood, they will die. A patient can be given a **blood transfusion** (someone else's blood put inside his or her body). Blood donors give blood, which is stored until it is needed. There are four different blood groups. If a person needs blood, he or she must be given the right blood group. If not, the body will reject it, and the patient could die.

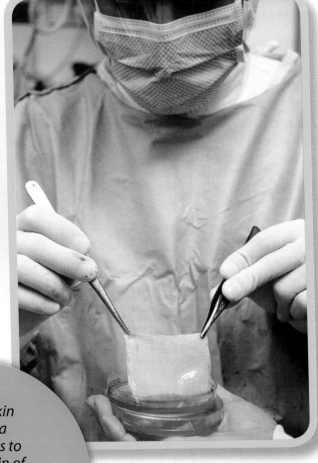

This human skin was grown in a laboratory. It is to replace the skin of a burn victim.

Organ donation

Damaged or diseased organs such as hearts, lungs, kidneys, livers, and skin can be replaced by a transplant. In most cases, organs can only be donated when someone (a donor) has died. <u>There are never enough donor organs for all the people who need them</u>. The body defenses of a patient who gets a new organ will try to reject and destroy it. These defenses are called the **immune system**. The patient will have to take drugs for the rest of his or her life to stop this from happening.

MICROSURGERY

Surgeons can now operate looking through magnifying lenses or even through a microscope. This lets them repair tiny blood vessels and nerves. It is called microsurgery. The thread that surgeons use to make stitches in microsurgery is so thin it can't really be seen just with the eyes.

Replacement microsurgery can reattach hands and other limbs.

Replacing lost limbs

One important use of microsurgery is to reattach limbs and other body parts that are lost in accidents. If the blood vessels and nerves can be joined together again, the person may be able to use a lost hand, finger, or toe almost as if it had never been damaged.

Different ways of moving

If surgery is not an option, many people still manage to lead active lives using wheelchairs and relatively simple artificial limbs to move around. Some people with artificial limbs can move faster than people who have their own legs!

Jeff Skiba of the United States is a high-jumper who has an artificial leg. He holds a world record for jumping 2.11 meters (6.92 feet).

Replacing lost faces

Some of the most amazing microsurgery has been achieved doing face transplants. Several people who had terrible injuries to their heads have been given a new face from dead donors. The patients can smile and show other feelings. The new face gives the patients a much better quality of life than before surgery.

Robotic limbs

Often lost limbs are so badly damaged they cannot be reattached. Modern artificial limbs can look very like the real thing. Computer technology means that soon artificial limbs may also be able to work as well as the real thing. Some new limbs are able to link to the nerves left in the end of the old limb. The new limb would then work the way the old one did.

Growing new organs

Scientists are working on growing new organs using special cells called **stem cells**. Stem cells can grow into almost any cell in the body. In 2010 scientists gave 11-year-old Ciaran Finn-Lynch a new trachea (windpipe) grown using his own stem cells. The new trachea is covered in Ciaran's own cells. His body defenses will not try to destroy it. So, he does not need to take drugs to stop his body from rejecting his new windpipe.

With a robotic arm like this, a person can open and close an artificial hand just by the power of thought.

TECHNOLOGY AT THE START OF LIFE

Most people assume they will be able to have a baby when they want one. <u>But one in every six couples has problems getting pregnant</u>. They have **infertility** issues. Advances in medical technology can help solve many of these problems.

In vitro fertilization

One common way of treating infertility is to use **in vitro fertilization** (IVF, or fertilization outside the body). **Eggs** are collected from the mother and mixed with **sperm** from the father outside the body. They combine to form **embryos**. An embryo is a baby at its earliest stage of development. One or two healthy embryos are then put back into the mother's body to grow and develop.

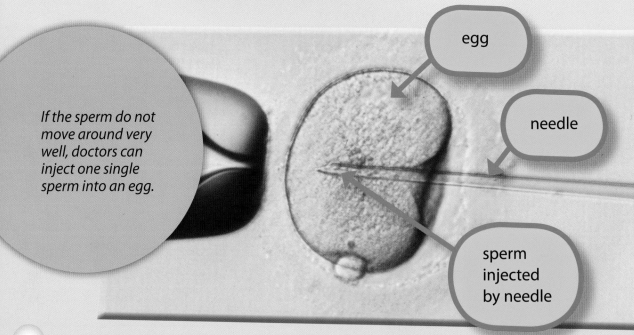

If the sperm do not move around very well, doctors can inject one single sperm into an egg.

egg

needle

sperm injected by needle

Freezing the future

For many years, doctors have been able to freeze sperm. Now they can freeze eggs and even embryos as well. This can help patients in many ways. For example, if young people need treatment for cancer, it could possibly make them incapable of having children. A young man needing cancer treatment can freeze sperm so that he can have children when he is older. A young woman can save her eggs before treatment.

Some women freeze their eggs so they can delay having a baby until they are older. Couples can save spare embryos made through IVF to have another child later on.

Inside the womb

The womb is the organ inside a woman's body where a baby develops. An embryo's development from a single cell is amazing. But things can go wrong. If a mother and baby have very different blood groups (see page 30), the mother's body may try to destroy the baby growing inside her. Doctors can give the baby blood transfusions inside the womb to keep it alive until it is born. Most operations on unborn babies are still very new and risky.

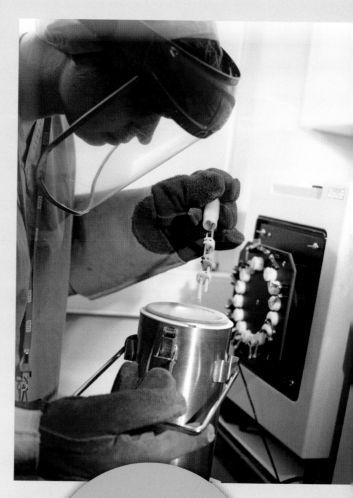

This technician is placing frozen human eggs in a container to transport them.

Twin success

Identical twins look exactly the same. They develop from a single fertilized egg. As they grow inside their mother, some can suffer from a condition called **TTTS**. This is where one twin gets more blood than the other. That twin becomes very big, and the other is very small. Often both babies die. Now, very successful surgery means doctors can change the blood vessels inside the womb, so that both babies grow normally.

WHO DID THAT?

U.S. surgeon Dr. Ruben Quintero figured out how to change the blood vessels and save the lives of twins with TTTS.

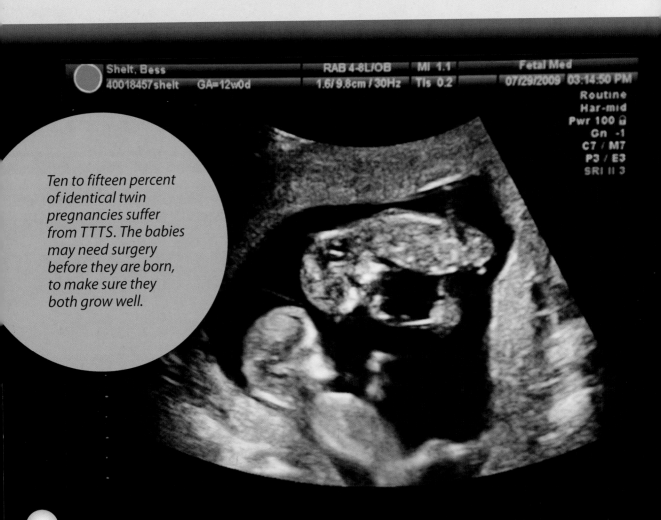

Ten to fifteen percent of identical twin pregnancies suffer from TTTS. The babies may need surgery before they are born, to make sure they both grow well.

Shelt, Bess
40018457shelt   GA=12w0d
RAB 4-8L/OB   MI 1.1   Fetal Med
1.6/ 9.8cm / 30Hz   TIs 0.2   07/29/2009 03:14:50 PM
Routine
Har-mid
Pwr 100
Gn -1
C7 / M7
P3 / E3
SRI II 3

Born too soon

A normal pregnancy lasts for around 37 to 42 weeks. A baby born much earlier than this is called **premature**. Premature babies often have many problems, because they are not fully formed. Their lungs don't work properly. They cannot control their body temperature. They cannot suck milk, so they cannot feed. Without special help, many of these babies die.

Incubators: An artificial womb

Incubators are special boxes that save the lives of many premature babies. They are placed over the baby's bassinet to keep it at the right temperature and supply it with extra oxygen. Incubators also check the baby's breathing and heart rate. Babies can be fed through tubes into their stomachs or even straight into their blood.

BRIGHT IDEA

Babies born before 30 weeks in the womb lack a special chemical called surfactant. This means their lungs can't stretch and fill with air easily. Scientists have developed ways to give surfactant to them. This helps their lungs to work normally, so they can survive.

It takes a lot of medical technology to save the life of a tiny premature baby.

NANOTECHNOLOGY AND GENETIC TECHNOLOGY

Nanotechnology works with material at the level of molecules. **Molecules** are the smallest parts that a substance can be broken into. This new technology uses very tiny particles (bits) that can only be seen with a special microscope called an electron microscope. Scientists are also looking at the molecules that make up the **genetic** code. This is called genetic technology. The genetic code is the information in the cells that controls how people look and how their bodies work.

Gold nanoparticles and cancer

Doctors are always looking for new ways to beat cancer. Cancer can grow in almost any area of the body. The chemicals used to treat cancer can often poison healthy cells as well. **Gold nanoparticles** are very small particles of gold. They are very useful. Gold does not react with other things in the body. But it can be joined to chemicals that are attracted to cancer cells. They can also be attached to cancer-killing drugs. Then the gold nanoparticles carry the drugs straight into the tumor.

Gold nanoparticles and heat

Gold is a metal. It heats up very easily. Once the gold nanoparticles are in the cancer cells, they can be heated up using lasers. They get hot enough to kill the cancer cells. This means doctors need to use fewer expensive drugs that can poison the body. Doctors hope using gold nanoparticles, drugs, and heat will become a very useful cancer treatment.

NANOBOTS AND NANOPROBES

In the future, doctors hope they will be able to use tiny machines called nanoprobes to find different diseases in the body. Then they will send tiny robots the size of molecules, called nanobots, into the blood. They will carry medicine to the right place or destroy damaged cells and cancer.

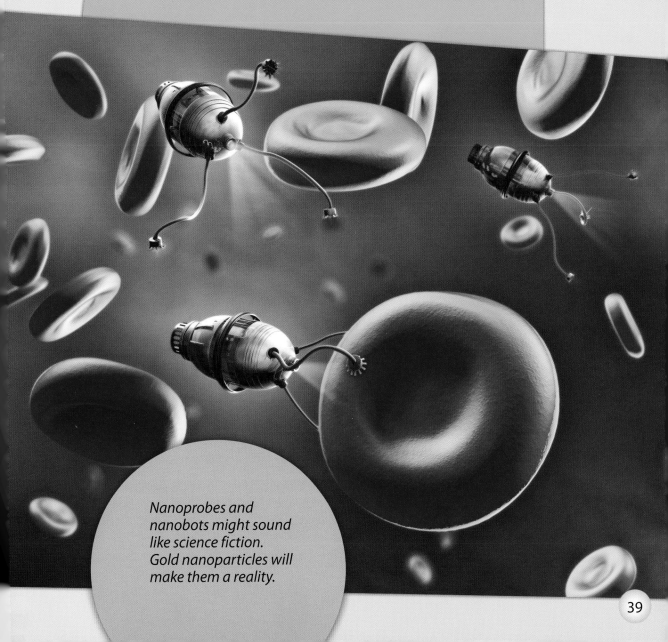

Nanoprobes and nanobots might sound like science fiction. Gold nanoparticles will make them a reality.

In the future, doctors may look at people's genetic codes to help diagnose their diseases. This will help doctors give the medicine that will work for patients.

Genetic medicine

Genes control what people look like and how their bodies work. Scientists have found genes for many different diseases. Some genes make people more likely to become sick. For example, some people have genes that mean they have a bigger risk of getting heart disease or cancer if they smoke. There are even genes that mean people have a high risk of getting breast cancer. Scientists have also found that people's genes affect how well different medicines work for them.

Genetic engineering

Scientists can cut a gene from one living thing and add it to the genetic material of another. This is called **genetic engineering**. For example, tiny living things called bacteria can be given the gene for human insulin. The bacteria then make pure human insulin, which is used to treat people with diabetes. Doctors and scientists also hope that one day soon, genetic engineering will be used to cure diseases caused by genes.

ENGINEERING A CURE

Some serious diseases such as cystic fibrosis and sickle cell anemia are passed from parents to children through their genes. Cystic fibrosis affects the lungs and digestive system, and sickle cell disease affects the blood.

In the future, with genetic engineering, we may be able to cut out healthy genes from the cells of a healthy person, and then insert them into the cells of a person with a genetic disease. This could keep them healthy for life.

Medical technology

Medical technology has come a long way. We can see deep inside the body using different types of scans. We can operate using scalpels, lasers, water, and ultrasound. We can replace damaged organs and limbs. We can operate through microscopes, using robots—even from one country to another.

The hospital of the future

Hospitals in the future may have no surgeries—just nano-surgeons injected into our blood to heal us. Our genes may be engineered before we are born, in order to remove the risk of many diseases. The medicine we are given will depend on our genes as well as our disease. No one knows. But medical technology will try to keep us healthy for many years to come.

TIMELINE

10,000–6,000 BCE (STONE AGE)	Trepanning, or simple brain surgery, is carried out without anesthetic.
1745 CE	The Company of Surgeons, which later becomes the Royal College of Surgeons, is formed in England.
1842	Dr. Crawford Long uses the chemical ether as an anesthetic for the first time.
1867	Joseph Lister recommends using phenol (carbolic acid) as an antiseptic (totally clean substance) in operating rooms. This substantially reduces the death rate from infections.
1895	X-rays are discovered by the German scientist Wilhelm Röntgen.
1896	X-rays are used in medicine to help set broken bones.
1902	The first successful kidney transplant on a dog is carried out.
1940s	Surgery to replace hip joints using artificial joints is developed.
1940s	Heart pacemakers are developed.
1953	The first heart–lung machine is developed by Dr. John Gibbon.
1954	The first successful human kidney transplant takes place in the United States, between identical twin brothers.
1959	Scottish doctor Ian Donald and his team develop ultrasound to diagnose problems in unborn babies.

1967	The first successful human heart transplant is carried out.
1970s	CAT scanners become widely used.
1977	The first full body MRI image is published.
1978	Louise Brown, the first baby to be conceived by IVF, is born.
1980	Lung surfactant is used on premature babies for the first time.
1990	Laparoscopic surgery is now used on children.
1991	The first robot surgeon operates on a person.
1998	Stem cells from embryos are grown in a laboratory for the first time.
2001	Laparoscopic surgery carried out on a woman in France is controlled by doctors in the United States.
2002	The first heart operation is carried out on a developing baby in the womb.
2005	The first partial face transplant is carried out in France using microsurgery.
2010	A surgical team successfully transplants a windpipe grown from his own stem cells into a boy.

Glossary

anesthesia loss of the sensation of touch or pain caused by drugs before surgery

anesthetic chemical that causes the loss of sensation of touch or pain during surgery

angiogram way of seeing the blood vessels of the heart by injecting a special liquid that shows up on X-rays

artery blood vessel carrying blood away from the heart. The blood usually contains lots of oxygen.

bacteria tiny living things that can cause disease

blood transfusion giving blood from one person to another

CAT scan scanner that uses X-rays and computers to make lots of clear images of slices through the body. Computers put all the information together to make a complete 3-D image.

cell tiny building block that forms all living things

CT scan see *CAT scan*

defibrillator device that uses an electric shock to restart a stopped heart

diagnose identify what is medically wrong with someone

diagnosis what is determined to be medically wrong with someone

dialysis process of using a special machine that takes over the work of the kidneys

egg female sex cell that joins with sperm to form an embryo, which may grow into a baby

electron microscope instrument that uses a stream of electrons to view things that are too small to be seen using a light. Electron microscopes magnify objects thousands of times.

embryo living thing in its earliest stages of development

endoscope tiny camera that can be put inside the body. It is used to spot problems and sometimes to perform surgery.

energy power, or the ability to do work

gene unit that controls a feature or part of a feature about you—for example, whether you have dimples

general anesthetic anesthetic that involves being put to sleep

genetic relating to genes

genetic engineering process in which the genetic material of a cell is changed by replacing damaged genes or adding extra genetic material

gold nanoparticle very tiny piece of gold that is effective in some medical treatments, such as treating cancer

HIFU (high-intensity focused ultrasound) type of ultrasound used in surgery that rapidly heats and seals blood vessels

immune system body system that acts as a line of defense against outside substances

infection when bacteria enter a body

infertility inability to produce offspring (babies)

in vitro fertilization (IVF) process in which eggs and sperm are combined outside the body to form an embryo. Healthy embryos are put into the mother's womb to grow.

laparoscopic surgery type of surgery in which the surgeon puts a tube containing a tiny camera through a patient's belly button. Surgical instruments go through tiny holes that are made.

laser beam of very bright light that contains lots of energy

life-support machine machine that takes over functions of the body

microorganism very tiny organism that can only be seen using a microscope

microsurgery surgery on very tiny blood vessels and nerves, performed through magnifying lenses or a microscope

molecule smallest part that a substance can be broken into

monoclonal antibody special substance that targets cells or chemicals in the body

MRI type of body scan that gives doctors a full picture of the inside of a body

nanotechnology science of using or making things that are about the size of molecules

premature born early. A premature baby is born after less than 37 to 38 weeks in the womb.

sperm male sex cell that joins with an egg to form an embryo, which may grow into a baby

stem cell cell that can grow into almost any other specialized type of cell in the body

stent metal mesh that is placed in a blocked artery to open it up and allow the blood to flow through

surfactant fluid in the lungs that keeps them open and expanded

surgeon doctor who performs operations

surgery opening up the body to remove parts that have a problem or to mend damaged tissue

trepanning early way of trying to cure seizures and headaches by making holes in the skull

TTTS (twin-to-twin transfusion syndrome) problem that can happen in identical twin pregnancies. One baby may receive more blood than the other. It becomes very big, while the other stays very small.

tumor lump of cancer cells

ultrasound sound that is too high for humans to hear

ultrasound scan way to produce pictures of organs inside the body using ultrasound

vaccine dose (often given as a shot) that "teaches" the body to fight off viruses and bacteria in the future

valve "door" in the heart that stops blood from flowing in the wrong direction

virus microorganism that causes disease and is infectious

Find Out More

Books

Fullick, Ann. *Science at the Edge: Frontiers of Surgery*. Chicago: Heinemann Library, 2006.
Read this book to explore the amazing technology used in surgeries of every kind.

Fullick, Ann. *Science at the Edge: Rebuilding the Body: Organ Transplantation*. Chicago: Heinemann Library, 2009.
This book explores the exciting medical technology that allows doctors to replace body parts, from parts of the eye to the heart and lungs.

Fullick, Ann. *Science at the Edge: Test Tube Babies: In Vitro Fertilization*. Chicago: Heinemann Library, 2009.
This book looks at the medical technology needed to overcome infertility.

Woods, Michael, and Mary B. Woods. *Technology in Ancient Cultures: Ancient Medical Technology: From Herbs to Scalpels*. Minneapolis: Twenty-First Century, 2011.
This book explores early kinds of medical technology—some of them a little scary!

Wyckoff, E. Britt. *Genius at Work: Heart Man: Vivien Thomas, African-American Heart Surgery Pioneer*. Berkeley Heights, N.J.: Enslow, 2008.
This book tells the story of Vivien Thomas, the great African American pioneer of heart surgery.

Websites

http://kidshealth.org/kid/
KidsHealth is a very useful website, covering all kinds of medical and health questions. Type topics of interest from this book—such as "heart disease" or "CAT scans"—to learn more about them.

www.pbs.org/wgbh/nova/heart/pioneers.html
Learn more about the history of heart surgery at this website.

www.spiritus-temporis.com/surgery/history-of-surgery.html
This History of Surgery website has a good and concise history of surgery and medical technology.

Places to visit

Most medical technology is kept and used in hospitals. When you have to visit your doctor or the hospital, keep your eyes open for whatever medical technology you can find.

International Museum of Surgical Science
1524 N. Lake Shore Drive
Chicago, Illinois 60610
www.imss.org

This museum is dedicated to the history, development, and advances of surgery. See fascinating displays and interactive exhibits.

Index